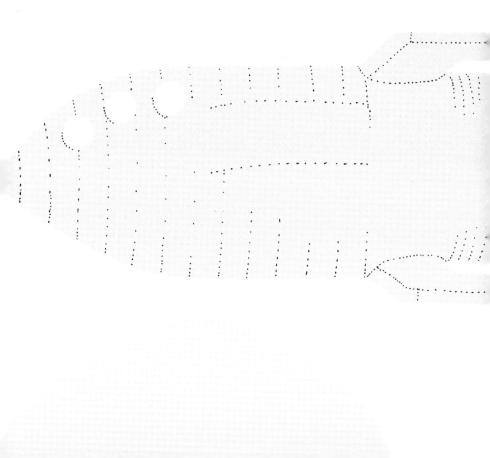

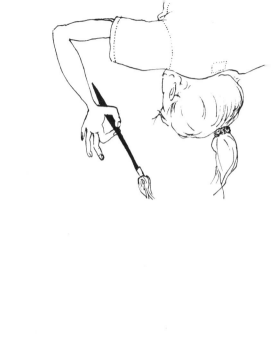

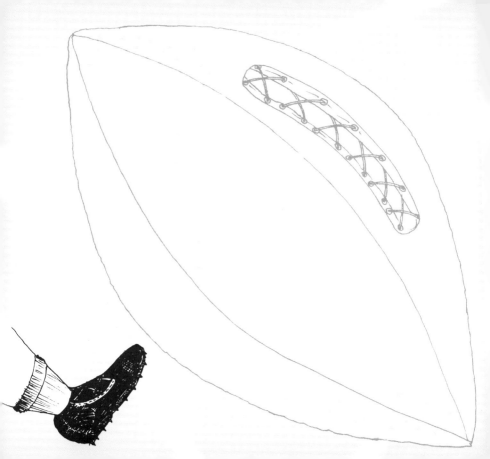

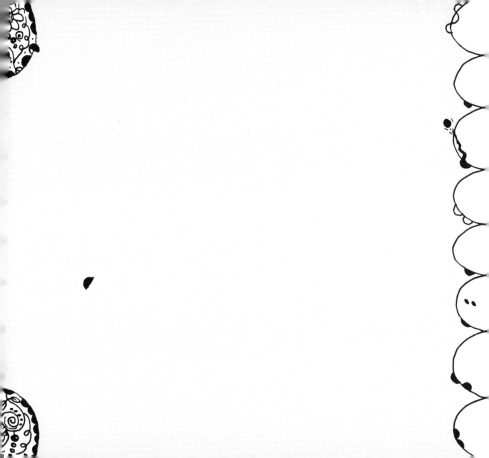

River

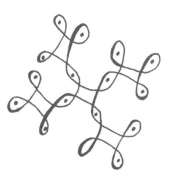

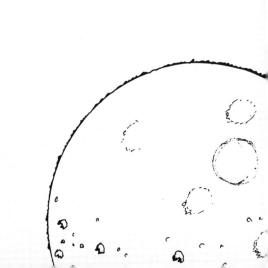

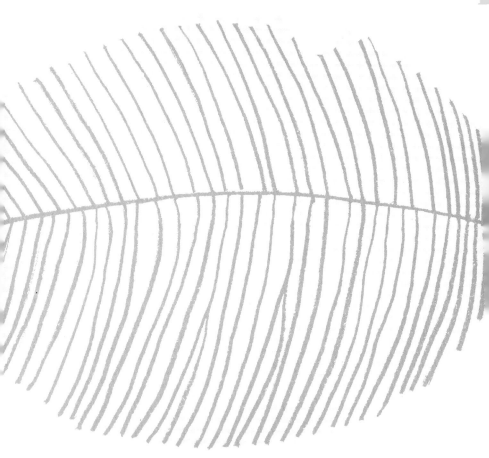

Use an opaque white pen to write here.

Silly & Sincere Doggerel Verses

**Make up your own, or use these when signing your friends' boo
and let your friends use 'em too in case they are wordless!**

☐ Roses R red,
     Violets are blue,
 R U 4 me?
      I M 4 U.

☐ U R A Q T

☐ 2 YS U R
   2 YS U B
   I C U R
   2 YS 4 me.

☐ Roses R red,
     Violets are blue,
   Sugar is sweet,
      And so are you.

☐ A cat has fur
     from tip to end,
 And I can purr,
      'cause you're my friend.

☐ If you're a frog I hop you'll live
         hoppily ever after.

☐ I M 4 U 24 7

☐ Today was tomorrow
     And will be yesterday,
 You're my friend forever,
      That's what I want to say.

☐ As time goes by,
     And, yes, time will,
 Remember your friend
    Who wrote uphill!

☐ I sign my name on this blue page,
   For you to read in your old age.

☐ Cardinals are wed,
Jays are bwue,
You're so tweet,
I wuv U 2.

☐ Hee hee hee, it makes me laugh,
To think you want my autograph.

☐ Yours 'til butter flies, . . . ice screams, . . .
cereal bowls, . . . hair cuts paper, . . .
the tree leaves, . . . the tree barks . . .

☐ Yum Yum!
I used a noodle
to do this doodle.

☐ Yours 'til the sand witch rides a broom.

☐ There are tulips in the garden,
There are tulips in the vase,
But the best tulips of all,
Are the two lips on your face!

☐ Can't think, can't rhyme,
Dry ink, it's time
To write that I'm
Your friend. The end.

☐ Remember me now, remember me ever,
Remember the fun we've had together.

☐ You catch a fish
with a hook;
You've caught me
in your book.

☐ What I'm told from morn to night
is that I oughta this, I oughta that
I oughta always do what's right.
So now my friend you oughta laugh,
'cause here I wrote my autograph.

☐ Here's my finger, here's my thumb,
Wave goodbye and I'll be glum.

☐ I like glop and I like goo,
You like me and I like you.

☐ Though I stay short, and you grow tall,
Our hearts don't' need to change at all.

☐ What is the end of E V E R Y T H I N G?
G. Gee! I'll miss you!

☐ X marks my spot,
don't rub is out.

☐ I like tacos, I like rice,
I like you! Olé, you're nice!

☐ Pirate ships . . . sunken ships . . .
There's no treasure ship like friendship.

☐ All I ask is one small spot •
in which to write, "Forget me not."

☐ This space is mine
wherein I write,
Remember me
when out of sight.

☐ Remember me when this you see,
And think of one who thinks of thee.

☐ I tried to write a rhyme,
But my brain won't help me out,
So I'll just say you're a friend of mine,
And that's without a doubt.

☐ Move your eyes from right to leftward,
Because ym eman I write backward.

☐ READ SEE HOW ME!
DOWN WILL I LOVE
AND YOU LOVE YOU
UP AND YOU IF

☐ My art and your heart
must never part.

☐ I sign upon this page of blue,
And hope your wishes all come true.

☐ You bring a book, I'll bring a pen,
Let nothing bring our friendship's end.

☐ Roses are red, blue is the sea,
I hope that you will remember me.

☐ A big fat kiss
to one I'll miss.

☐ Same old story, nothing new—
It always starts with "I like you"
And always ends with "We are friends."

☐ Cuckoo, peacock, chicken, crow,
You're the tweet heart I want to know.

☐ Do I love you, or do I not?
I told you once, but I forgot.

☐ Jack be nimble, Jack be fast,
Our friendship will always last.

☐ I write on the right
so I won't be left!

☐ What has many leaves . . . but no stalk,
Lots of words . . . but can't talk?
This book.

☐ FRIEND spelled with one letter is U.

☐ The winds did whine,
     The leaves did fall,
   Here is my sign,
     And that is all.

Some write up and some write down, but all be different, and all write around!

☐ Remember A
     Remember B
   And C that U
     Remember me.

☐ Don't get me wrong,
     Just let me write,
   A little song,
     To sing tonight.

☐ Say well and do well,
     End with one letter,
   Say well is good,
     Do well is better.

☐ I can't be in 12 places,
     With only one behind,
   That's why there's only one place
     Where you will find I signed.

☐ When for me you pine,
     Just look at my sign.

☐ Best friends we are,
     Best friends we'll be,
   Best friends forever — you and me.

☐ U R U and I M ME
   and U and I makes WE.

· Dot
  Blot
  Forget-
  me-
  not

Rhyming Words

(useful <u>almost rhyming</u> words are in parentheses)

NAME acclaim aim blame came fame flame frame game same tame
(brain chain drain gain insane main pain plain rain sane train twain)

ALBUM bum chum come cranium crumb drum dumb fi-fi-fo-fum glum
gum hum humdrum medium mum numb plum some sum thumb tum-tum
(grumble tumble)

AUTOGRAPH behalf half giraffe laugh phonograph

BOOK cook crook hook look shook took

CLASS alas bass gas glass grass lass mass pass sass (fast last past)

DAY away clay delay hey may neigh pay play ray say stay yay

DAYS amaze daze gaze maze phrase praise raise

EVER clever forever never sever (feather forgetter leisure measure
pleasure together treasure weather whether)

FRIEND bend blend end lend mend send tend (pen them then when)

HEART apart art chart depart part smart start wart

INK   clink drink link pink sink stink think

PAGE   age cage engage gage gauge rage sage stage

PAPER   caper scraper shaper vapor (eraser flapper greater nature wrapper)

POEM   "owe him" (ahem dome foam gem gnome home pome roam stem them tome um)

SIGN/SIGNED   combine design Einstein fine incline intertwine line mine nine pine porcupine shine spine valentine vine whine wine — behind blind find grind hind kind mind remind

VERSE   nurse purse rehearse reverse terse worse (burst first thirst worst)

WORD/WORDS   absurd bird blurred curd furred heard herd nerd stirred whirred (mirrored world worst)

WRITE   appetite bite bright delight fight flight fright height kite might night quite right sight tight unite white

WRITTEN   bitten "fit in" hittin' kitten mitten quittin' sittin'

WROTE   anecdote boat devote float note quote throat vote

YEAR   appear cheer clear dear deer ear fear hear near rear sincere sphere tear